Piano

Commissioned by and Dedicated to Kent L. Leslie

THE GLASS BEAD GAME

Concerto for Horn and Orchestra

After Hermann Hesse

Solo Horn with Piano Reduction

By JAMES A. BECKEL Jr.

Piano reduction edited by Sheryll McManus

HAL•LEONARD®
CORPORATION
7777 W. BLUEMOUND RD. P.O. BOX 13819 MILWAUKEE, WI 53213

About The Composer

Mr. Beckel graduated from the Indiana University School of Music and has been the Principal Trombonist with the Indianapolis Symphony since 1969. He is also on the music faculty at DePauw University and the University of Indianapolis. In addition to these responsibilities he has been a very active composer and arranger. Mr. Beckel was born in Marion, Ohio in 1948.

Many original works have been performed by several professional orchestras such as Minneapolis, St. Louis, Atlanta, Houston, Cincinnati, Baltimore, Detroit, Milwaukee, Indianapolis, Rochester, Charlotte, Fort Wayne, Rhode Island, Springfield, Evansville, Tampa, Arkansas, Oklahoma City, Terra Haute, South Bend, Omaha, Knoxville, Delaware, West Virginia, etc.

Mr. Beckel has received many composition grants. He has been an Individual Arts Fellow through the Indiana Arts Commission and the National Endowment for the Arts, and recently was one of 50 composers chosen nationwide to be part of the *Continental Harmony Project*. "Liberty for All" was written for that commission from *Composers Forum*. "The Glass Bead Game" was nominated for a Pulitzer Prize. "The Glass Bead Game: Concerto for Horn and Orchestra" was premiered by the Indianapolis Chamber Orchestra on November 10, 1997. Kent Leslie was the horn soloist. "The Glass Bead Game" is now available with orchestra, wind ensemble, piano, and chamber ensemble written for piano, harp, and percussion. Mr. Beckel has also written several works for brass choir and brass quintet. Other works written by the composer include:

"Night Visions"	*A four movement programmatic work for orchestra.*
"The American Dream"	*A patriotic overture written for orchestra. This work is also available for concert band from Hal Leonard Corporation.*
"Waltz of the Animals"	*A children's work for orchestra and narrator.*
"Celebrations"	*A jazz pops overture for orchestra.*
"A Christmas Fanfare"	*A Christmas overture for orchestra. Also available for brass choir.*
"A Gospel Christmas Medley"	*A medley of Gospel songs arranged for orchestra.*
"Freedoms Hope"	*A work for brass quintet and optional percussion.*
"Musica Mobilis"	*A work for brass choir.*
"A Christmas Medley"	*A medley of Christmas songs for brass septet.*
"Three Sketches for Orchestra"	*A three movement work for orchestra featuring jazz trombone soloist.*
"Amazing Grace"	*An arrangement of this hymn favorite for orchestra with optional choir and vocal soloist available for sale from the Indianapolis Symphony Orchestra library.*
"Liberty for All"	*A patriotic work for symphony orchestra and narrator.*

All works are listed with B.M.I. Inquiries contact Mr. Beckel at Musbeck @MSN.com

About the Work

"The Glass Bead Game" is a horn concerto loosely based on the Herman Hesse novel of the same title. This work is programmatic in nature while following the basic concerto form. In the first movement, two main themes dominate. The work opens with a bi-tonal motif based in E♭ major and A major. This musical idea is meant to represent Herman Hesse's existential philosophy about life, which is reflected in his novel. Simply put, Hesse believed that man exists as an individual in a purposeless universe that is basically hostile. This conflict between man and his environment is represented by the juxtaposition of the two keys. His main character of this novel in fact succumbs to the cold waters of a glacier-fed lake at the end of this book. The other main theme is a leitmotif representing the main character, Joseph Knecht; and is first stated by the solo horn at letter A of the first movement. The dialogue of this theme between horn, flute, and piccolo was inspired by the introduction of the Music Master in this novel. Joseph Knecht meets the Music Master, who accepts our main character into the intellectual society of the elite Castalia.

The second movement is dedicated to Father Jacobus. While the first movement leitmotif for Joseph Knecht was based on 5ths going up; Father Jacobus' leitmotif is based on 5ths going down. The second movement makes much use of sounds sustained into each other, as you would hear in a Great Cathedral. The movement is meant to reflect the peace that Joseph Knecht felt with the introduction of history and religion.

The final movement is the most programmatic. This movement begins with the opening celebration of Joseph Knecht's coronation to the post of Magister Ludi. The celebration is heard at first from a great distance. Since Joseph Knecht is reticent about his promotion to this high post, the horn soloist, representing our main character, never plays the *Celebration March* melody. The solo horn instead answers the melody with protest. This opening section of the final movement eventually grows to a frenzy introducing us finally to the *Presto* theme featuring the solo horn. The theme from the second movement is briefly referenced at letter Mm as Joseph Knecht, now burdened with the responsibilities of the Magister Ludi, reflects on his more tranquil past at the monastery with Father Jacobus. At the close of this movement, the drowning sequence is loosely reflected in the music when the opening themes of the third movement return as our main character drowns.

Opening thematic material to the second movement is used as transition to return us to the original Joseph Knecht leitmotif at letter Rr in this final movement. Programmatically this is referencing the end of this great novel where Joseph Knecht's student, Tito, is now sitting on the lake's shore in shock over the death of his teacher, Joseph Knecht. But our main character lives on in Tito's mind as a wonderful teacher and mentor.

Comissioned by and Dedicated to Kent L. Leslie

THE GLASS BEAD GAME

Concerto for Horn and Orchestra

After Hermann Hesse

By JAMES A. BECKEL Jr.
Piano reduction edited by Sheryll McManus

Performance Time: 20:00

1st Movement: *The Call and Awakening*

*Eighth notes remain constant throughout the 1st movement.

R **Andante ala Recitative** (♩ = 60)

2nd Movement: *Father Jacobus*

Commissioned by and Dedicated to Kent L. Leslie

THE GLASS BEAD GAME

Concerto for Horn and Orchestra

After Hermann Hesse

Solo Horn with Piano Reduction

By JAMES A. BECKEL Jr.

Piano reduction edited by Sheryll McManus

HAL•LEONARD®
CORPORATION
7777 W. BLUEMOUND RD. P.O. BOX 13819 MILWAUKEE, WI 53213

About The Composer

Mr. Beckel graduated from the Indiana University School of Music and has been the Principal Trombonist with the Indianapolis Symphony since 1969. He is also on the music faculty at DePauw University and the University of Indianapolis. In addition to these responsibilities he has been a very active composer and arranger. Mr. Beckel was born in Marion, Ohio in 1948.

Many original works have been performed by several professional orchestras such as Minneapolis, St. Louis, Atlanta, Houston, Cincinnati, Baltimore, Detroit, Milwaukee, Indianapolis, Rochester, Charlotte, Fort Wayne, Rhode Island, Springfield, Evansville, Tampa, Arkansas, Oklahoma City, Terra Haute, South Bend, Omaha, Knoxville, Delaware, West Virginia, etc.

Mr. Beckel has received many composition grants. He has been an Individual Arts Fellow through the Indiana Arts Commission and the National Endowment for the Arts, and recently was one of 50 composers chosen nationwide to be part of the *Continental Harmony Project*. "Liberty for All" was written for that commission from *Composers Forum*. "The Glass Bead Game" was nominated for a Pulitzer Prize. "The Glass Bead Game: Concerto for Horn and Orchestra" was premiered by the Indianapolis Chamber Orchestra on November 10, 1997. Kent Leslie was the horn soloist. "The Glass Bead Game" is now available with orchestra, wind ensemble, piano, and chamber ensemble written for piano, harp, and percussion. Mr. Beckel has also written several works for brass choir and brass quintet. Other works written by the composer include:

"Night Visions"	*A four movement programmatic work for orchestra.*
"The American Dream"	*A patriotic overture written for orchestra. This work is also available for concert band from Hal Leonard Corporation.*
"Waltz of the Animals"	*A children's work for orchestra and narrator.*
"Celebrations"	*A jazz pops overture for orchestra.*
"A Christmas Fanfare"	*A Christmas overture for orchestra. Also available for brass choir.*
"A Gospel Christmas Medley"	*A medley of Gospel songs arranged for orchestra.*
"Freedoms Hope"	*A work for brass quintet and optional percussion.*
"Musica Mobilis"	*A work for brass choir.*
"A Christmas Medley"	*A medley of Christmas songs for brass septet.*
"Three Sketches for Orchestra"	*A three movement work for orchestra featuring jazz trombone soloist.*
"Amazing Grace"	*An arrangement of this hymn favorite for orchestra with optional choir and vocal soloist available for sale from the Indianapolis Symphony Orchestra library.*
"Liberty for All"	*A patriotic work for symphony orchestra and narrator.*

All works are listed with B.M.I. Inquiries contact Mr. Beckel at Musbeck @MSN.com

About the Work

"The Glass Bead Game" is a horn concerto loosely based on the Herman Hesse novel of the same title. This work is programmatic in nature while following the basic concerto form. In the first movement, two main themes dominate. The work opens with a bi-tonal motif based in Eb major and A major. This musical idea is meant to represent Herman Hesse's existential philosophy about life, which is reflected in his novel. Simply put, Hesse believed that man exists as an individual in a purposeless universe that is basically hostile. This conflict between man and his environment is represented by the juxtaposition of the two keys. His main character of this novel in fact succumbs to the cold waters of a glacier-fed lake at the end of this book. The other main theme is a leitmotif representing the main character, Joseph Knecht; and is first stated by the solo horn at letter A of the first movement. The dialogue of this theme between horn, flute, and piccolo was inspired by the introduction of the Music Master in this novel. Joseph Knecht meets the Music Master, who accepts our main character into the intellectual society of the elite Castalia.

The second movement is dedicated to Father Jacobus. While the first movement leitmotif for Joseph Knecht was based on 5ths going up; Father Jacobus' leitmotif is based on 5ths going down. The second movement makes much use of sounds sustained into each other, as you would hear in a Great Cathedral. The movement is meant to reflect the peace that Joseph Knecht felt with the introduction of history and religion.

The final movement is the most programmatic. This movement begins with the opening celebration of Joseph Knecht's coronation to the post of Magister Ludi. The celebration is heard at first from a great distance. Since Joseph Knecht is reticent about his promotion to this high post, the horn soloist, representing our main character, never plays the *Celebration March* melody. The solo horn instead answers the melody with protest. This opening section of the final movement eventually grows to a frenzy introducing us finally to the *Presto* theme featuring the solo horn. The theme from the second movement is briefly referenced at letter Mm as Joseph Knecht, now burdened with the responsibilities of the Magister Ludi, reflects on his more tranquil past at the monastery with Father Jacobus. At the close of this movement, the drowning sequence is loosely reflected in the music when the opening themes of the third movement return as our main character drowns.

Opening thematic material to the second movement is used as transition to return us to the original Joseph Knecht leitmotif at letter Rr in this final movement. Programmatically this is referencing the end of this great novel where Joseph Knecht's student, Tito, is now sitting on the lake's shore in shock over the death of his teacher, Joseph Knecht. But our main character lives on in Tito's mind as a wonderful teacher and mentor.

Comissioned by and Dedicated to Kent L. Leslie

THE GLASS BEAD GAME
Concerto for Horn and Orchestra
After Hermann Hesse

Solo Horn in F

By JAMES A. BECKEL Jr.
Piano reduction edited by Sheryll McManus

Performance Time: 20:00

1st Movement: *The Call and Awakening*

* Eighth notes remain constant throughout the 1st movement.

Andante Recitative (♩ = 54)

Attacca to 2nd Movement

2nd Movement: *Father Jacobus*

* Dotted slurs indicate a phrase.

Attacca to 3rd Movement

3rd Movement: *Magister Ludi Coronation and Death*

* At the discretion of the soloist, letter Uu to the end may be performed offstage without mute.

* Dotted slurs indicate a phrase.

Attacca to 3rd Movement

3rd Movement: *Magister Ludi Coronation and Death*

* At the discretion of the soloist, letter Uu to the end may be performed offstage without mute.